W9-AVX-245

# MONTANA
## WILD AND BEAUTIFUL II

PHOTOGRAPHY BY CHUCK HANEY AND JOHN REDDY

FARCOUNTRY
PRESS

RIGHT: Bowman Lake in Glacier National Park.
JOHN REDDY

TITLE PAGE: Hellgate Gulch keeps an ice floe chilled
in the Big Belt Mountains.
JOHN REDDY

ENDPAPERS, BACKGROUND ON PAGES 1, 4, 5:
Grass on Mullan Pass.
JOHN REDDY

*On the dust jacket*
FRONT: Looking past beargrass blossoms
onto Grinnell Lake, Glacier National Park.
CHUCK HANEY

BACKGROUND: Snow pattern.
JOHN REDDY

FRONT FLAP: Cloud study in the Big Sky.
JOHN REDDY

BACK: Springtime in Lewis and Clark County.
JOHN REDDY

ISBN 1-56037-231-1

© 2002 Farcountry Press

Photographs © by individual photographers as credited

This book may not be reproduced in whole or in part by any means (with the excep-
tion of short quotes for the purpose of review) without permission of the publisher.
For more information on our books call or write: Farcountry Press, P.O. Box 5630,
Helena, MT 59604, (406) 443-2842 or (800) 654-1105,
or visit our website: www.montanamagazine.com

Created, designed, and published in the USA. Printed in China.

2

*E*very spring the fervor happens all over again as I pour over dog-eared pages of my Montana map collection. They lie across my office floor like a jigsaw puzzle as I attempt to piece together another season's shooting schedule. From the broad scope of the atlas to the contour lines of a topographical map to the tearsheets of some obscure article I've stuffed away, I tend to daydream about a portion of Montana that hasn't had my tripod legs imprinted into it yet. The bug to explore new terrain in a larger-than-life landscape has taken hold of me once again.

Where else can you spend the morning photographing the "Running of the Sheep" Festival from a roof top in Reedpoint, then later in the evening watch the antics of a family of prairie dogs at Greycliff State Park? I've had days that began in the cool shade of a rainforest environment like Avalanche Gorge in Glacier National Park, and ended with reddish hues of last light striking precariously balanced badlands rocks.

Recently, I explored the sparsely populated northeast corner of Montana. I cruised long miles of gravel roads, dirt roads, and roads that could pass for trails. All these arteries led me to an ocean of green prairie grasses dotted with water-filled potholes that attracted thirsty birds under that famous big blue sky. This expansive setting produced the sense of freedom found only in such remote places. Yes, out in the Big Sky Country of Montana, a man has time to ponder, to inhale the fresh sage-scented air, and to enjoy the satisfaction of wanting to be nowhere else.

I must admit: I'm extremely lucky! I love whom I'm with, what I do, and where I live. I get the rare opportunity to explore my home state at the most beautiful times and experience its home-grown culture firsthand. There's something special about witnessing events like the state basketball tournaments or track competitions where high school kids adorned in a rainbow of school colors come from seemingly every corner of our vast state to compete. From Plentywood to West Yellowstone, Montana produces terrific kids.

The ghost town of Dooley, in northeastern Montana.
CHUCK HANEY

Attending the tiny Fourth of July parade in the frontier-like community of Polebridge, where electric lines and smooth roads have yet to reach, still puts a lump in my throat when the whole crowd breaks into patriotic songs. Taking in a Native American pow-wow celebration—hearing the traditional songs, seeing the friendly faces, and eating the frybread—is one of highlights of any year. There can be nothing more American or Montanan than events like these.

You may have noticed that I haven't mentioned much about the actual pursuit of taking the photographs. I'll let the following pages do the talking. For me, just being alive in Montana drives the passion to capture a small slice of my beloved state on film. Seeing fantastic landscapes in perfect light, and meeting interesting folks along the way, form a wondrous way of life!

Maybe I should ask for a new set of maps this Christmas. I'm certain that I will never run out of intriguing subjects to photograph.

*C.H.*

These days, advances in photographic technology are so rapid that it seems you can't keep up with them from day to day. First there was auto-focusing, which is ancient history now. Then there were digital cameras, scanners, ink-jet printers, light-jet printers, micro-drives.... There are even cameras that focus by detecting the movement of the human eye and lenses that compensate for an unsteady hand, thereby minimizing the need for a tripod. With computer software like Photoshop and others, it can be difficult to tell if the picture you are looking at is 100% real. Distracting elements can be removed and missing ones added. Colors can be enhanced. No doubt, someday photographic film will be obsolete. The digital imaging boom is in a frenzy! Of course this is all a reflection of our modern impatient society. We must have it now…no time to wait!

There are people everywhere who think that if they have all the latest camera equipment their pictures will be the best. I see this when teaching workshops. These photographers buckle under the weight of huge camera bags, overflowing with the latest gear, and field vests with every pocket filled, while staring intently at thick owner's manuals! They are so preoccupied with all this complex equipment that they miss what's going on around them. For me, what it's really about is looking in that viewfinder and getting rid of what doesn't belong. In-camera editing. Simple!

This is a book about what Montana looks like. Well, it looks like a lot of different things depending on where you are in the state, what time of year it is, if it's midday or sunrise, sunny or overcast. Montana is big and it's diverse. The weather constantly keeps us guessing. What a great place to live! So, next time you're out and about, don't fuss with all the details—you might miss the splendor that's all around you in Montana.

*J.R.*

Swiftcurrent Falls carries chilly snow-melt in Glacier National Park.
JOHN REDDY

ABOVE: Along the Yellowstone River near Sidney, this year's wheat crop flourishes.
CHUCK HANEY

FACING PAGE: West Fork Rock Creek, in the Sapphire Mountains.
JOHN REDDY

ABOVE: Disking a field as autumn arrives near Lewistown.
CHUCK HANEY

RIGHT: Parker Homestead State Park near Three Forks protects a sod-roofed homestead cabin.
CHUCK HANEY

ABOVE: This juvenile bobcat will never be anyone's kitty.
JOHN REDDY

LEFT: Lupine along Jacobson Creek in the Pioneer Mountains.
CHUCK HANEY

ABOVE: Morning light brings out the details of Medicine Rocks State Park in the southeast.
CHUCK HANEY

RIGHT: Wahkpa Chu'gn bison kill site at Havre shows how Indians harvested bison before they received horses.
CHUCK HANEY

FACING PAGE: Willow Creek runs through a Valley County ranch near Hinsdale.
CHUCK HANEY

Blanketflowers' yellow and sticky geraniums' pink accent the Many Glacier Valley, Glacier National Park.
CHUCK HANEY

ABOVE: Patrolling the Ninepipe National Wildlife Refuge, a male ring-necked pheasant.
CHUCK HANEY

RIGHT: Ross Creek in northwestern Montana's Kootenai National Forest.
CHUCK HANEY

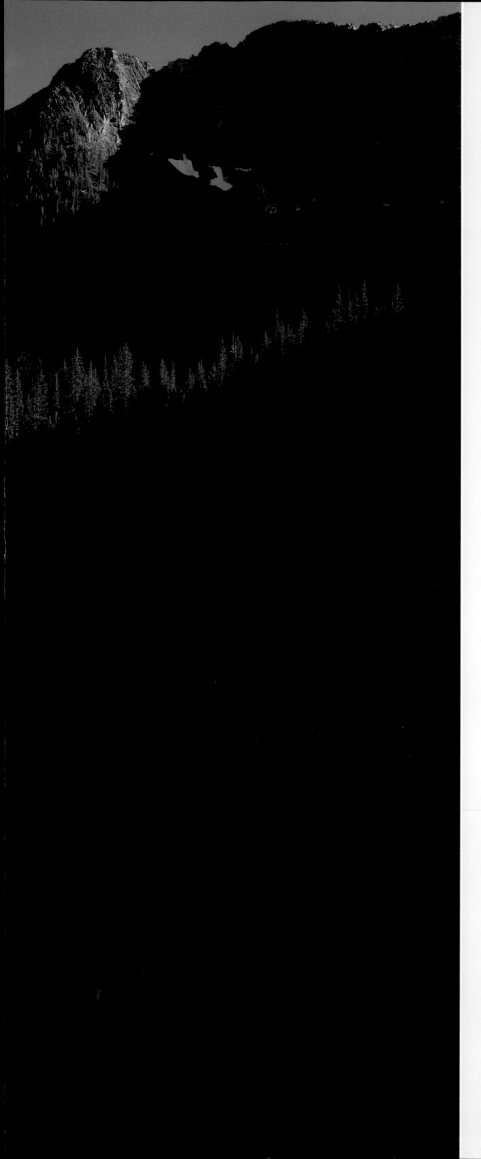

ABOVE: Trying a fly on Ninemile Creek near Huson.
CHUCK HANEY

LEFT: Big Johnson Lake in the Anaconda–Pintler Wilderness Area.
JOHN REDDY

ABOVE: Swan Range from Holland Lake outlet.
JOHN REDDY

RIGHT: Fort Peck Lake on the Missouri River offers plenty of elbow room for fishing.
CHUCK HANEY

FACING PAGE: End of a winter day at Hot Springs.
CHUCK HANEY

ABOVE: Cleveland-area ranch.
CHUCK HANEY

LEFT: A beaver lodge in the Big Hole valley's Miner Lake.
JOHN REDDY

Moonrise over rimrocks near Winnett.
CHUCK HANEY

ABOVE: At a "lek," a site where males show off their charms, this sage grouse hen prepares to select her mate.
CHUCK HANEY

RIGHT: Glacier National Park's Cut Bank Valley below Mad Wolf and Bad Marriage mountains.
CHUCK HANEY

ABOVE: The observation tower at Medicine Lake National Wildlife Refuge witnesses hundreds of thousands of birds passing by each year.
CHUCK HANEY

LEFT: A big welcome in the seat of Powder River County.
CHUCK HANEY

FACING PAGE: North Fork of the Flathead River near Columbia Falls.
CHUCK HANEY

ABOVE: A Glacier National Park waterfall turns abstract.
JOHN REDDY

FACING PAGE: Rainy Lake is one of the Swan Valley's jewels,
with the Swan Range on the horizon.
JOHN REDDY

ABOVE: Yes, the little yellow fuzzball will grow up to look just like mama Canada goose.

JOHN REDDY

LEFT: Devils Glen on the Dearborn River, near the Rocky Mountain Front.

JOHN REDDY

33

ABOVE: Cottonwood trees along the Marias River in their exuberant autumn dress.
CHUCK HANEY

RIGHT: Billings, Montana's largest city.
CHUCK HANEY

LEFT: The Terry Badlands' Red Cliffs, further colored by sunset's glow.
CHUCK HANEY

BELOW: The Yaak River flowing among larch trees in the fall.
CHUCK HANEY

ABOVE: Hoarfrost on trees and bushes along the Missouri River.
JOHN REDDY

FACING PAGE: The Sapphire Mountains' Skalkaho Falls.
JOHN REDDY

ABOVE: Taking a break at the Hargrave Ranch near Marion.
CHUCK HANEY

LEFT: Spring reaches into the Big Hole after a mild winter.
JOHN REDDY

ABOVE: Columbian ground squirrels are lively rodents.
CHUCK HANEY

RIGHT: A foggy sunrise at Gates of the Mountains on the Missouri River near Helena.
JOHN REDDY

ABOVE: Awaiting its dancer at a Fort Missoula powwow.
JOHN REDDY

LEFT: Evening light on the Marias River near Shelby.
CHUCK HANEY

ABOVE: Charolais beef cattle below the Rocky Mountain Front.
JOHN REDDY

RIGHT: Ross Creek cedars in northwestern Montana's Bull River Valley.
JOHN REDDY

FACING PAGE: A summer storm over Glacier National Park
approaches St. Mary Lake.
JOHN REDDY

ABOVE: Cold and peaceful Swiftcurrent Lake in Glacier National Park.
JOHN REDDY

FACING PAGE: The Gallatin River, which joins the Jefferson and the Madison in Montana to form the Missouri River.
JOHN REDDY

ABOVE: This Swainson's hawk is ready to hunt in the Centennial Valley.
JOHN REDDY

RIGHT: Dusk over the gold- and silver-rich Flint Creek Range.
JOHN REDDY

ABOVE: Kayaking the Gallatin River.
JOHN REDDY

LEFT: A prairie dog whistles the alarm for its "town."
CHUCK HANEY

FACING PAGE: Limestone cliffs form Trout Creek Canyon
in the Big Belt Mountains.
JOHN REDDY

ABOVE: Whitewater rafting is one way to tour the Middle Fork of the Flathead River.
CHUCK HANEY

RIGHT: Electric Peak (rising to 10,994 feet) is in the Montana portion of Yellowstone National Park.
JOHN REDDY

LEFT: An Elkhorn Hot Springs guest cabin's welcoming glow.

JOHN REDDY

BELOW: Below the Tobacco Root Mountains on a late-summer day, hay bales on tidy display.

JOHN REDDY

FACING PAGE: Makoshika State Park was named from the Sioux for "bad land."

JOHN REDDY

ABOVE: Steeple detail of St. Mary's Mission, Stevensville.
JOHN REDDY

RIGHT: Egg Mountain near Choteau is one of the world's prime dinosaur fossil sites.
CHUCK HANEY

ABOVE: Hyalite Creek's Grotto Falls drops through the Gallatin Mountains near Bozeman.
JOHN REDDY

LEFT: Looking across Ninepipe Reservoir to the Mission Mountains.
JOHN REDDY

ABOVE: Dawn over Lake McDonald, Glacier National Park.
JOHN REDDY

RIGHT: These iron sculptures by Blackfeet artist Michael Kevin Hope are part of his group of thirteen that tell the Blackfeet creation story, and can be seen throughout Browning.
CHUCK HANEY

FACING PAGE: Destroyed in a 1960s modernization effort, the stained-glass barrel-vault skylight over the main staircase was recreated in time for the Montana capitol's centennial in 2002.
JOHN REDDY

Aspens' autumn glory in Lewis and Clark National Forest.

JOHN REDDY

65

ABOVE: Near Miles City, a wintry sunset on the Yellowstone River.
CHUCK HANEY

RIGHT: The Jerusalem Rocks, fantastically shaped sandstone formations, stand near Sweetgrass.
CHUCK HANEY

ABOVE: Pronghorns—wrongly called antelopes—are built for short bursts of high-speed running to elude danger.
CHUCK HANEY

LEFT: Skunk cabbage marks the emergence of spring in Flathead National Forest.
CHUCK HANEY

FACING PAGE: In the Kootenai National Forest.
JOHN REDDY

ABOVE: Snow patterns at Park Lake.
JOHN REDDY

RIGHT: Horse halters—decoration courtesy
of Jack Frost.
JOHN REDDY

FACING PAGE: Glacier National Park's Garden
Wall above McDonald Creek.
JOHN REDDY

ABOVE: Fancy fencing and a fine new roof in the Big Hole.
CHUCK HANEY

LEFT: Magic light on Culbertson-area prairie.
CHUCK HANEY

ABOVE: The Swan Valley and the Clearwater River.
JOHN REDDY

TOP: Rainbow Lake, near Plains.
CHUCK HANEY

FACING PAGE: The Cabinet Mountains' Ross Creek Falls.
JOHN REDDY

LEFT: The Madison River, a Missouri River tributary, near West Yellowstone.
JOHN REDDY

BELOW: Happiness for a moose is a delicious pond-bottom buffet.
CHUCK HANEY

ABOVE: St. Peter's Roman Catholic Church in Wibaux was faced with lava rock when built in 1895.
CHUCK HANEY

FACING PAGE: Apikuni Falls and Creek in Many Glacier Valley, Glacier National Park.
CHUCK HANEY

ABOVE: Enjoying Crow Fair parade at one of the nation's largest powwows, held each year at Crow Agency.
CHUCK HANEY

FACING PAGE: The Child–Kleffner barn near East Helena dates from 1888.
CHUCK HANEY

ABOVE: Refrigerator Canyon in the Gates of the Mountains Wilderness
Area offers a cool respite even on summer's hottest days.
JOHN REDDY

RIGHT: Fishing 'til the light dies on the Bull River in Sanders County.
CHUCK HANEY

ABOVE: Missouri River sunset at Great Falls.
CHUCK HANEY

LEFT: Pompeys Pillar National Monument near Billings holds William Clark's signature, carved in 1806 as the Lewis and Clark Expedition headed home.
CHUCK HANEY

FACING PAGE: "Snow ghosts"—pine trees wrapped in fresh snow—high above Whitefish.
CHUCK HANEY

ABOVE: Atop Mullan Pass, on the Continental Divide northwest of Helena.
JOHN REDDY

RIGHT: Up close at a Little Belt Mountains barn.
JOHN REDDY

FACING PAGE: Ford Creek's Double Falls on the Rocky Mountain Front, where the Rockies abruptly meet the Great Plains.
JOHN REDDY

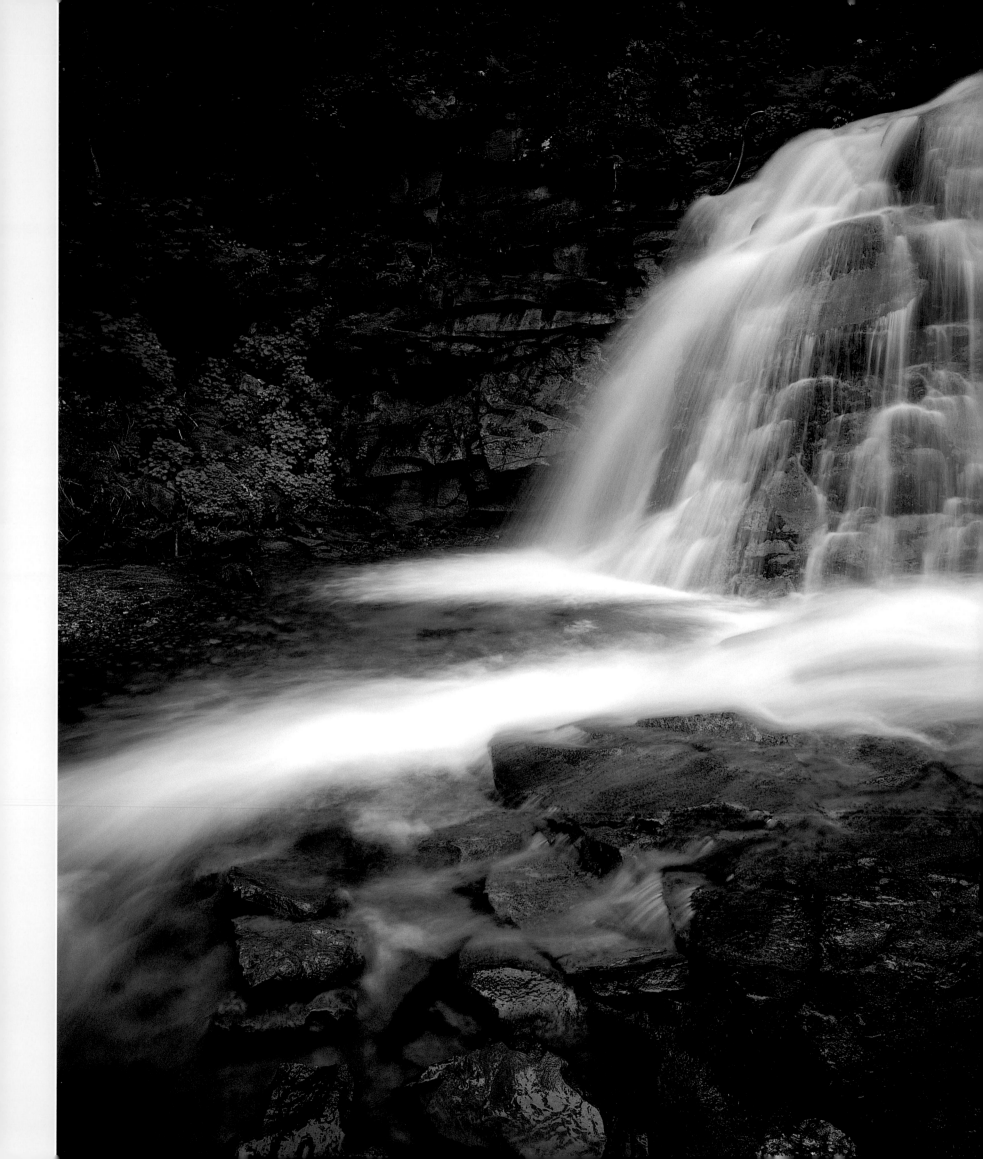

ABOVE: Biking the trails up Mount Helena City Park is one way to get a great view of the city and St. Helena's Cathedral.
CHUCK HANEY

LEFT: The Crazy Mountains, near Big Timber, at dawn.
CHUCK HANEY

RIGHT: Grizzly bears are often called "silvertips" because of their hair's frosted look.
CHUCK HANEY

BELOW: Domestic ewes and lambs near Big Timber, part of the 360,000 that rank Montana seventh among sheep-producing states.
CHUCK HANEY

FACING PAGE: Avalanche Creek surrounded by fresh snow in Glacier National Park.
CHUCK HANEY

ABOVE: Wolf Creek–area survivor.
JOHN REDDY

LEFT: Dusty Star Mountain and St. Mary Lake, Glacier National Park.
JOHN REDDY

BELOW: Snowflakes fill the air during morning feeding near Ovando.
CHUCK HANEY

ABOVE: "Copper King" Marcus Daly's mansion, Riverside,
is now open to the public at Hamilton.
CHUCK HANEY

RIGHT: The Shoshone Indians named Beaverhead Rock, and Sacagawea
recognized this landmark near today's Dillon as she returned to her
homeland with the Lewis and Clark Expedition.
CHUCK HANEY

ABOVE: Bracken fern's autumn gold.
CHUCK HANEY

TOP: Red Angus calves, further tinted by sunset light,
on a Valley County ranch.
CHUCK HANEY

LEFT: Arrowleaf balsamroot blooms above Dickey Lake
in northwestern Montana.
CHUCK HANEY

ABOVE: The Rocky Mountain Front between Augusta and the Dearborn River.

JOHN REDDY

RIGHT: Iceboaters enjoy Canyon Ferry Lake on the Missouri River, in Broadwater County.

CHUCK HANEY

FACING PAGE: Looking from Beartooth Pass to the Beartooth Plateau in Montana's highest mountain range.

JOHN REDDY

LEFT: Hard at work.
JOHN REDDY

BELOW: McDonald Creek tones.
JOHN REDDY

FACING PAGE: Springtime in the Centennial Valley.
JOHN REDDY

ABOVE: Wind-sculpted snow along the Rocky Mountain Front.
JOHN REDDY

RIGHT: Reflections on the Beartooth Plateau near Red Lodge.
CHUCK HANEY

ABOVE: Red Rock Lakes National Wildlife Refuge.
JOHN REDDY

FACING PAGE: Fall color on the lower Garden Wall, Glacier National Park.
JOHN REDDY

A storm clears away from Seeley Lake.
JOHN REDDY

ABOVE: The Big Belt Mountains hold these pictographs by ancient residents.
JOHN REDDY

RIGHT: Snowmobiling near West Yellowstone, the "Snowmobile Capital of the World."
CHUCK HANEY

FACING PAGE: Beautiful but ominous sky over the Prickly Pear Valley.
JOHN REDDY

ABOVE: Hell Creek State Park sandstone formation near Jordan.
CHUCK HANEY

LEFT: Canoeing the White Cliffs area of the Wild and Scenic Missouri River.
CHUCK HANEY

ABOVE: The Blackfoot River in spring.
CHUCK HANEY

RIGHT: Bighorn sheep ram.
CHUCK HANEY

FACING PAGE: Granite rocks rise from
the Continental Divide near Butte.
JOHN REDDY

ABOVE: This cougar is hard at work.
JOHN REDDY

RIGHT: Storm-reversed light on a hay field near Whitefish.
CHUCK HANEY

ABOVE: Mountain goat kids check out trail hikers in Glacier National Park.
CHUCK HANEY

RIGHT: Haystack Butte near the Rocky Mountain Front.
JOHN REDDY

ABOVE: Amtrak's *Empire Builder* is a fine way to see the Northern Rockies.
CHUCK HANEY

FACING PAGE: Southeastern Montana's stretch of the Bighorn River in Bighorn Canyon National Recreation Area.
JOHN REDDY

FOLLOWING PAGE: Day's end over St. Mary Lake.
JOHN REDDY